MW00892204

Dear Participant:

In 2009 CCAR developed the Recovery Coach Academy© out of a need for our volunteers to develop their skills and understanding of recovery in order to help those who were coming into our centers seeking help for their own addictions. What was built out of a way for our volunteers to give back to those in recovery sparked a movement in peer support services. The CCAR RCA took the Recovery Community by storm. So much so, that we can proudly say that to date (September 2017) CART has trained nearly 20,000 coaches in our CCAR curriculums.

CART is dedicated to building training programs to support this movement so that coaches are able to regularly refine their craft of actively listening, asking good questions and managing their own stuff. Because of these high standards of excellence for our training programs and expectations of what we feel make good Recovery Coaches, CART is constantly asked to help agencies looking to employ CCAR trained Recovery Coaches. However, the landscape of where those roles are available has changed. Typically you'd find Recovery Coaches at your local recovery community centers, but now we are seeing a greater need for skilled coaches to work in other professional settings, such as hospitals, treatment facilities, police stations and court systems. In response to the demand, CART has developed what we think will be a highly utilized and sought-after training program for Recovery Coaches looking to work or are working within professional settings.

Participants in this training will:

- Define professionalism as it pertains to recovery coaching;
- Learn about and develop the various characteristics that a professional possesses;
- Understand their personal accountabilities in their role as recovery coaches;
- Learn the importance of the concept "stay in their lane" when it comes to working in a large system, like a hospital, court and/or treatment system;
- Reexamine the roles of a recovery coach in order to maintain good boundaries when working in professional settings;
- Have opportunities to practice and demonstrate newly acquired skills.

We wish you well.

CART Staff

This CCAR Training Manual is meant to accompany your participation in the CCAR program bearing the same name. Instruction is to be provided by an authorized CCAR Facilitator, with a CEU Award provided for the successful completion. For this purpose we track attendance and participation in Protraxx, CCAR's Professional Development Tracking Platform.

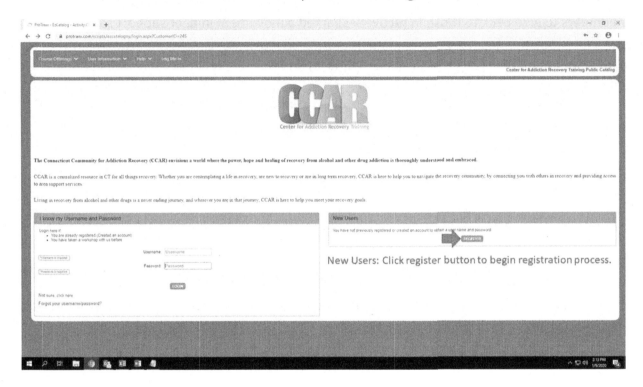

New Users: Click register button to begin registration process.

Please note: CCAR Utilizes a Professional Development Platform called PROTRAXX to track all your classes, evaluations and CEU awards. You should have received a link from your CCAR Facilitator to enroll in this platform. If you have not done this necessary step, please speak with your facilitator during a break so you will receive full credit for this class.

Day One

9:00 a.m. to 12:00 p.m.	Welcome
	Introductions
	Overview of the Program/Working Agreements
	What is Professionalism?
	BREAK
	Accountability
	Appearance Part 1
	Lunch
1:00 p.m. to 4:00 p.m.	Journaling
	Appearance Part 2
	Etiquette
	BREAK
	Communication

Facilitator Expectations

Working agreements are guidelines developed by a group of people regarding how they will work together to create a positive, productive process. Working agreements describe desired behaviors you would like all members of the group to follow.

As facilitators, we encourage you to have:

- A willingness to allow each person to share without fear of judgment or ridicule.
- Open-mindedness towards fellow members' beliefs and opinions as they are shared during the course.
- A willingness to be vulnerable about your beliefs and attitudes.
- An enthusiastic hope that we'll all complete this program wiser and more accepting than when we started.

For this course, the agreed upon working agreements will be posted for reference through the two days of training.

Professionalism

Before we can talk about Professionalism in Recovery Coaching, we need to know what it means to be a professional.

List characteristics that a professional possesses below?

Given the list of characteristics, how would you define the word professionalism?

_____

_____

_____

_____

_____

_____

Given the definitions that were just shared, what do you feel are Assets and Liabilities when working as a Recovery Coach Professional?

Assets/Pros	Liabilities/Cons

According to Merriam-Webster,

Professionalism is defined as:

the conduct, aims, or qualities that characterize or mark a profession or a professional person

Professional is defined as:

exhibiting a courteous, conscientious, and generally businesslike manner in the workplace

In your groups, take a few moments to write down the answer to this question:

Is it important to be seen as a professional when working in certain settings as a Recovery Coach? Why?

Accountability

In the last section we spoke a bit about assets and liabilities of being a Recovery Coach Professional, let's go a bit deeper and identify who we serve.

In your groups please list the people/groups you serve as a Recovery Coach, and how they view recovery coaching.

Who do we serve as Recovery Coaches?	What are some attitudes this group might express about recovery coaching?

How would you prioritize this list?

Appearance

Please rate on a scale of 1-10 how would you rate these recovery coaches on the following:

Characteristics?								
Accountable								
Reliable								
Organized								
Polite, Courteous								
Competent								
Approachable								
Ethical								
A good communicator								
Totals:								

Based on the total, who would appear to be the most professional?

You never get a second chance to make a first impression – in fact your first impression is based on how others 'see' you, and less about what you say or how you say it.

Facts:
- o Words only account for 7% of an initial impression
- o Vocal quality (your tone of voice) accounts for another 38%
- o 55% accounts for non-verbal perception of appearance and behavior

To that end, what does a professional appearance, or dress code, look like for Recovery Coaches?

ABC Services is in the process of hiring Recovery Coaches. Take a few moments to write down what should be included in their dress code for this new group of coaches.

(You may use the internet, sample requirements, etc., to help generate a list.)

There are a variety of dress codes out there – casual, business casual, business attire – it's hard to know what is acceptable and what isn't.

Sample Dress Codes

Casual:
Dark denims
Tasteful Sneakers
Nice plain T-shirts
Casual collared shirts (polos)
Fitted blouses/button downs
Sweaters
Business Casual:
Shirts and sweaters in a variety of colors/patterns
Slacks or khakis
Combinations of blouses/buttons downs, vests
Skirts (fingertip length)
Relaxed shoes
Business Attire:
Dress Slacks/Skirts (knee-length)
Button down shirts
Sports coat, Cardigan
Suit
Dress shoes, loafers, pumps (low heel)

While you will want to dress in a way that connects to the people you serve, these are some thoughts to consider when deciding on what to wear in your role as Recovery Coach:

- Think about the environment: Is it safe to wear long earrings, open toed-shoes, etc.
- Make sure you have cleaned trimmed nails, facial hair.
- Does the organization where I will be providing services allow tattoos, piercings?
- As you will be in close proximity to others, make sure your teeth are clean, breath is fresh. Always use deodorant, but beware of heavy perfumes or colognes.
- Choose clothes that are cleaned and pressed. Refrain from wearing t-shirts with graphics, sports teams, jeans/pants with tears/holes, and hats (baseball or knit caps).
- Refrain from wearing clothes that reveal undergarments (e.g. bra straps, low pants that show underwear, etc.)

Agencies may have their own dress codes, so you should always adhere to their stated rules.

Etiquette

When we hear a term like etiquette, it can oftentimes be thought of as old fashioned. Or, you may be reminiscent of the term "Miss Manners" and keeping your elbows off the table at dinner time. The term etiquette is simply a code of behavior. Having proper etiquette simply demonstrates having respect and being considerate of others. The etiquette of business is the set of written and unwritten rules of conduct that make interactions run more smoothly. Office etiquette in particular applies to coworker interaction, and the way you interact with the people you serve in your role as Recovery Coach.

Think about the following scenarios that may arise when serving as a coach.

1. A recoveree fails to arrive to a meeting at the scheduled time. When they arrive late, they still want to meet. What do you do:

    a. Thank them for making it in and have the session.
    b. Tell them you no longer have time to meet and ask them to reschedule with the receptionist.
    c. Ask why they are late and explain the consequences of their actions.

2. When corresponding with someone via email, it is a good idea to begin it with a formal greeting, e.g. good afternoon

                    True   False

3. It is acceptable to have your cell phone set to ring during appointments.

                    True   False

4. When meeting your recoveree for the first time, you should reach out and give them a hug.

                    True   False

5. A co-worker shares gossip with you about another co-worker.

    Do you:

a. Thank them for telling you
b. Check out the facts with your supervisor
c. Politely listen
d. End the conversation

6. When speaking to someone on the phone who is saying the same thing over and over.

Do you:

a. Politely interrupt and ask how you can assist.
b. Tell them you can't help them and put them on hold and tell your supervisor.
c. Hang up.

7. After a first meeting with a recoveree it's ok to text to their personal phone, stating how exciting you are to begin working with them.

                    True   False

8. You are being introduced to the recoveree's family,

Do you:

a. Stand up and shake hands
b. Smile and nod
c. Wave and say how happy you are to meet them.

9. You have a scheduled meeting with your supervisor at 10:00. It is now 10:05 and you haven't been invited into their office yet.

Do you:

a. Leave a post it on their door saying to come find you when they are finished.
b. Knock and say, "Excuse me, did you forget about our meeting?"
c. Sit and keep waiting.

10. A new recoveree is being oriented to your place of employment, a colleague walks by using colorful language about another recoveree. What do you do?

a. Politely apologize and lead the new person out of the area.
b. Ask the person who is swearing to watch their language.
c. Say, that's how things get around here sometimes, and continue to show them around.

Think of and write down a scenario that depicts poor etiquette by a Recovery Coach.

In your small groups, brainstorm a list of good etiquette.

Communication

Communication is a key factor in our role as Recovery Coaches. In our role we will communicate with many different people, including the people we are coaching, members of their family/support system, supervisors, team members, other coaches, and the recovery community to name a few. What we say is just as important as how we say it. This next module will discuss multiple ways to communicate as well as how to communicate in a professional manner.

Here is a good list of skills need to communicate effectively.

10 Communication Skills that Demonstrate Professionalism

1. **Listening** - Being a good listener is one of the best ways to be a good communicator. No one likes communicating with someone who only cares about putting in her two cents, and does not take the time to listen to the other person.
2. **Nonverbal Communication** - Your body language, eye contact, hand gestures, and tone all color the message you are trying to convey. A relaxed, open stance (arms open, legs relaxed), and a friendly tone will make you appear approachable, and will encourage others to speak openly with you.
3. **Clarity and Concision** - Good communication means saying just enough - don't say too little or talk too much. Try to convey your message in as few words as possible. Say what you want clearly and directly, whether you're speaking to someone in person, on the phone, or via email.
4. **Friendliness** - Through a friendly tone, a personal question, or simply a smile, you will encourage your coworkers to engage in open and honest communication with you. It's important to be nice and polite in all your workplace communications. This is important in both face-to-face and written communication.
5. **Confidence** - It is important to be confident in all of your interactions with others. Confidence ensures your coworkers that you believe in and will follow through with what you are saying. Exuding confidence can be as simple as making eye contact or using a firm but friendly tone (avoid making statements sound like questions). Of course, be careful not to sound arrogant or aggressive.
6. **Empathy** - Even when you disagree with an employer, coworker, or employee, it is important for you to understand and respect their point of view.
7. **Open-Mindedness** - A good communicator should enter any conversation with a flexible, open mind. Be open to listening to and understanding the other person's point of view, rather than simply getting your message across. By being willing to enter into a dialogue, even with people with whom you disagree, you will be able to have more honest, productive conversations.

8. **Respect** - People will be more open to communicating with you if you convey respect for them and their ideas. Simple actions like using a person's name, making eye contact, and actively listening when a person speaks will make the person feel appreciated. On the phone, avoid distractions and stay focused on the conversation.

9. **Feedback** - Being able to appropriately give and receive feedback is an important communication skill. Accept, and encourage, feedback from others. Listen to the feedback you are given, ask clarifying questions if you are unsure of the issue, and make efforts to implement the feedback.

10. **Picking the Right Medium** - An important communication skill is to simply know what form of communication to use. People will appreciate your thoughtfulness and will be more likely to respond positively to you.

What is your experience with some of the methods we have shared?

Which ones are you gifted at?

Where can you improve?

Phone Etiquette –

- When calling someone, be prepared, identify yourself, the business, reason for the call.
- Be conscious of other's time.
- Note the time of day you are calling
- When leaving a message, leave full name, number and reason for the call.
- Return voicemails within one business day,
- When answering calls, identify yourself immediately
- Try not to put callers on hold for more than a few seconds
- If you are not the right person, let the person know who you are transferring them to – along with a number in case you get disconnected.
- Avoid personal calls, especially in shared spaces.

Day Two

9:00 a.m. to 12:00 p.m.	Welcome and Reacquaintance
	Review of the Program/Working Agreements
	Reliability
	Boundaries, Part 1
	BREAK
	Boundaries, Part 2
	Demeanor
	Lunch
1:00 p.m. to 4:00 p.m.	Journaling
	Maintaining Poise
	Organization
	BREAK
	Competence
	Closing/Evaluation

How Reliable am I?

Please rate yourself the following statements:

	Always 1	2	Sometimes 3	4	Never 5
I am often asked to take on additional tasks/responsibilities.	○	○	○	○	○
When I am asked to do something, I do it right away.	○	○	○	○	○
Once I set my mind to complete something, I do it.	○	○	○	○	○
I make sure that anything I take the time to do is done without errors.	○	○	○	○	○
I am asked to assist others often.	○	○	○	○	○
When I am asked to take on more responsibilities, I am open to taking on the additional work.	○	○	○	○	○
Co-workers can depend on me to be on time and ready to get started, regardless of the task.	○	○	○	○	○
When I accept an invitation I attend the events.	○	○	○	○	○
Close friends, family, or co-workers describe me as trustworthy.	○	○	○	○	○
I keep my word when I promise to do something.	○	○	○	○	○
When I am asked to complete something in a pre-determined timeframe, I do.	○	○	○	○	○
I won't take on anything I cannot handle, and will ask for help when I need it.	○	○	○	○	○
I answer my phone and return calls promptly.	○	○	○	○	○
I am prepared for meetings and or presentations I am scheduled to give.	○	○	○	○	○
When participating in a team project, I do my fair share of the work, do it well and on time.	○	○	○	○	○
I return email and text messages within a timely manner	○	○	○	○	○

A reliable person is someone who you can trust to behave well, work hard, or do what you expect them to do. In our work as Recovery Coaches, we have an obligation or "accountability" to be reliable to the people we coach, our recoverees. When we work in professional settings, we also need to be reliable to the people who are part of our organization, our team and our managers.

Ways to be reliable in the workplace:

- Keep your word
- Be consistent
- Honor your commitments
- Arrive to work on time (and be ready to work)
- Follow through – finish your work when you say you will, show up when you say you will and help when you make the offer to assist others.

Describe the importance of reliability?

How does being reliable demonstrate professionalism in our work?

Taking a page out of the RCA, take a few moments to write a SMART goal for yourself that would improve your reliability.

Remember the characteristic of a SMART Goal are:

Specific	Define Expectations. Avoid generalities and use verbs to start the sentence
Measurable	Establish concrete criteria for measuring progress toward the attainment of each goal you set. Quality, Quantity, timeliness.
Achievable	Challenging goals within reason. Do not assign too many goals though each one is within reason
Realistic	A goal must represent an objective toward which you are both willing and able to work. A goal can be both high and realistic.
Time-Bound	Date or elapsed time to complete the goal

Goal

Steps I need to take to reach my goal

Who else might be involved?

When do I want to have this goal accomplished?

Boundaries

There is often a lack of clarity around professional and personal boundaries for Recovery Coaches. We would like to explore that for a bit by asking you to list factors that help you to delineate the difference between Professional and Personal relationships.

Professional Relationships	Personal Relationships

Given the lists that we generated earlier, generate a scenario that would be personally challenging; where the lines of a professional and personal relationship are blurred.

Boundary Basics for Professionals

One aspect of ethics, professionalism and overall wellness is maintaining healthy boundaries.

- Boundaries protect the coach, the recoveree, family members, your employer, and the recovery community.

- Develop a recovery-based decision making process that is deeper than "Is this right or wrong?"

- Consider all parties who may be affected in any situation.

- Your employer's code of conduct, if any, must become second nature.

- When in doubt check it out with a supervisor and/or other recovery coaches.

For additional information, please review an article by William White (White, W., the PRO-ACT Ethics Workgroup, with legal discussion by Popovits R. & Donohue, B. (2007). Ethical Guidelines for the Delivery of Peer-based Recovery Support Services. Philadelphia: Philadelphia Department of Behavioral Health and Mental Retardation.)

Professional	Personal
• More boundaries	• Less boundaries
• More power differential	• Less power differential
• More work conversations	• More family conversations
• Conditional relationship	• Unconditional relationship
• More skepticism	• Less skepticism
• More privacy	• Less privacy
• Less conversation about politics, church	• More conversations about politics, church
• Less trust	• More trust
• Less intimacy	• More intimacy
• Less recreation	• More recreation
• Less accessible	• More accessible
• Friendly	• Friendships
• Less emotional	• More emotional
• Less vulnerability	• More vulnerability
• Forced	• Chosen

Demeanor

Being a Recovery Coach Professional is demonstrated in the way we handle ourselves in certain situations.

> **According to Merriam-Webster,**
>
> **Demeanor is defined as:**
>
> *behavior toward others: outward manner*

To demonstrate a professional demeanor...

- Stay calm and cool in tense situations
- Be positive
- Be accountable
- Have a sense of humor
- Be humble

Do not...

- Complain and/or vent
- Lose your temper
- Argue with co-workers/manager

Laurie the Nurse

Laurie is a nurse at the Emergency Room you are assigned to work in. She is constantly complaining about all the "gomers*" that keep taking up beds in her ER. You hear her making negative comments to other staff members about your role, the people you are serving and how these people are never going to get better so "Why do we even have Recovery Coaches?"

*Get out of my Emergency Room

How do you respond to this situation?

Sam the Coach

Sam was just informed that a few co-workers have called out sick, and he is the only one to handle the day's caseload. At first, everything goes well but quickly spirals out of control. Sam has three face to face requests for visits from different hospitals, two calls on hold, and is talking to a distressed family member. A new recoveree bursts into the small office and demands to speak to Sam immediately.

How does Sam respond to this situation?

Maintaining Poise

This training has taken us through the attributes of what makes a professional recovery coach. In this next section we would like you to put your training into Action....as in Lights, Camera, Action!

Develop a skit - portrayal or parody - of a chaotic Emergency Room Department where a Recovery Coach maintains his/her poise (or not). Showcase some of the examples we have learned about the following: Communication, Etiquette, Demeanor, Ethics, Appearance, Accountability and Reliability.

Each person should have a role in the skit – even if it is a non-speaking role. Use the space below to write any notes about your parody.

Organization

When working in a professional setting, it is not enough to appear professional; you also need to work like a professional.   Having good organizational skills is a way to demonstrate your skills and capacity as a Recovery Coach Professional.

Take this assessment to determine if you are as organized as you'd like to be.

1.	True	False	I can find anything I need in two minutes or less.
2.	True	False	I feel in control of my space, time, and papers.
3.	True	False	Cleanup is quick because I know where everything goes.
4.	True	False	I am rarely late.
5.	True	False	I rarely lose things.
6.	True	False	Getting ready to go out is a smooth process.
7.	True	False	Procrastination is rarely a problem for me.
8.	True	False	I get my work done on time and am pleased with the results.
9.	True	False	I feel happy with what I accomplish every day.
10.	True	False	I rarely hear myself apologizing for how my workspace looks.
11.	True	False	I am comfortable in my workspace.
12.	True	False	I think being disorganized is an obstacle to my success.

If you answered "False" to 3 or more of the above questions, you have room for improvement when it comes to your organizational skills. Continuing to work on these skills will prove to be very helpful in increasing your level of achievement and reducing your stress.

Organization Improvement Worksheet

First, pick a part of your life where you feel organization could be improved (i.e. your desk, workspace, house, etc.)

Your area for improvement:_____

Question 1: What's working and what's not?

What's working:

1.　　I can always find my_____

2.　　I always have a place to put my_____

3.　　I like the current set-up of my_____

4.　　No matter how busy I get, I always find time for_____

5.　　My goals are well defined when it comes to_____

What's not working:

1.　　I can never find my _____

2.　　I have no place to put my_____

3.　　I don't have enough time for_____

4.　　I procrastinate whenever I have to_____

5.　　I have a hard time finishing_____

Question 2: What's your essential 7?

What are the 7 most important items in the area you are about to organize?

(i.e. what are the objects you are constantly looking for and need most often?)

1.	5.
2.	6.
3.	7.
4.	

Question 3: What's the pay-off?

What are the reasons why it will be worthwhile to get organized in this area?

1._____

2._____

3. _____

Question 4: What can I do better to organize in this area?

The Eisenhower Matrix

The Eisenhower Matrix, also referred to as Urgent-Important Matrix, helps you decide on and prioritize tasks by urgency and importance, sorting out less urgent and important tasks which you should either delegate or not do at all.

	URGENT	NOT URGENT
IMPORTANT	**DO** Do it now. Write article for today.	**DECIDE** Schedule a time to do it. Exercising. Calling family and friends. Researching articles. Long-term biz strategy.
NOT IMPORTANT	**DELEGATE** Who can do it for you? Scheduling interviews. Booking flights. Approving comments. Answering certain emails. Sharing articles.	**DELETE** Eliminate it. Watching television. Checking social media. Sorting through junk mail.

"What is important is seldom urgent and what is urgent is seldom important."
-Dwight Eisenhower, 34th President of the United States

We call the first quadrant "Do" as its tasks are important for your life and career and need to be done today or tomorrow at the latest. You could use a timer to help you concentrate while trying to get as much of them done as possible.

The second quadrant we call "Decide". Its tasks are important but less urgent. You should list tasks you need to put in your calendar here.

The third quadrant is for those tasks you could "Delegate" as they are less important to you than others but still pretty urgent. You should keep track of delegated tasks by e-mail, telephone or within a meeting to check back on their progress later.

The fourth and last quadrant is called "Delete" because it is there to help you sort out things you should not be doing at all.

There is an additional Time Management Checklist on page 38 – feel free to also assess these skills in your free time.

Competence

The definition of competence is having the necessary ability, knowledge, or skill to do something successfully. One way to demonstrate professionalism in your role as a Recovery Coach is to strive to perfect your craft, by both attending training programs such as this one and practicing your ART.

What are some ways we can demonstrate competency (knowledge, skills and abilities) in our role as Recovery Coach?

Why is it important to demonstrate this to others?

Taking a page out of the RCA, take a few moments to write a SMART goal for yourself that would support your growth as a recovery coach professional.

Goal
Steps I need to take to reach my goal
Who else might be involved?
When do I want to have this goal accomplished?

If we do all of this well- we expect to be well received and welcomed!

Evaluation and CEU Award

Congratulations! As you have registered in CCAR's Protraxx System you will receive and email shortly after the conclusion of this class with a unique link to complete your evaluation. This step is necessary to obtain your CEU Award for this CCAR Training Program. Once you have completed the evaluation your Protraxx Dashboard will automatically populate with your award.

- You can view your award, or save it by clicking on the "My enrollments" tab on the menu bar.

- This will bring up a listing of all CCAR activities attended.

- You can then click on the View Award Icon.

- Once the award is open click the file icon to save or print.

- If you have forgotten your user name or password, or need assistance retrieving your award, please visit www.addictionrecoverytraining.org/protraxx

If you have not registered or enrolled in the Protraxx platform, please connect with your CCAR Facilitator.

Additional Resources

The Etiquette Code: Requirement or Just a Guideline?
By Ryan Underwood
Youth Development and Leadership Consultant
TRI Leadership Resources

In Disney's Pirates of the Caribbean we learn about the "Pirates Code." Johnny Depp's famous character Captain Jack Sparrow challenges his crew to "keep to the code." Then, we learn later from Keira Knightly's character Elizabeth that the sacred code "is more like a guideline anyway."

Since before the days of pirates, there has been a professional code that those who desire success, acceptance, and good fortune have subscribed. In the 1700's the French defined this code as the word "etiquette." Etiquette originally described the rules for how to behave at court with kings and queens. Today we know etiquette in many forms from business and dining to and golf and even cell phones.

Society may seem more informal than they were in days of kings and queens and even pirates. It appears we live in a more casual and relaxed time. With all the new innovations making our lives so fast paced, do we still have time old rules of etiquette? Do we need still need manners or is being nice enough? Is the code of etiquette "required" or "just a guideline anyway"?

Rest assured, etiquette lives! While the etiquette guidelines change from setting to setting and even from country to country, the rules of manners, decorum, and what Mom would call "your best behavior" are alive and well and required now more than ever.

Think of etiquette as the outer expression of the inner leader. Your outer professionalism is an indicator of your inner excellence. Practicing good etiquette demonstrates you are willing to make small sacrifices of personal comfort and pleasure in order to make others feel warm, welcome, and included. If you care about the details of decorum you tell the world you also care about the details of projects, initiatives, and assignments—and naturally people will want you on their team, group, and on board their leadership!

There are many courses, books, and trainings to learn about etiquette. Learning the "etiquette code" is the first step toward practicing the code. Search Amazon.com and you'll find a virtual treasure chest full of great resources on the subject.

Not many know that George Washington lost his father when he was just 11 years old. As a young student, Washington wrote 110 Rules of Civility & Decent Behavior in Company and Conversation as a homework assignment. It was said of America's first President, "no wonder everyone honored him who honored every body." President Washington's 110 rules might be overwhelming to start with, so, we've boiled down the rules of etiquette to 10 basics to get you started.

Remember the Etiquette Code

1. **Remember Your ABCs!** Always Be Caring, Comforting, and Courteous. Honor others with respect and it will flow to you, your family, your team, and those you associate.

2. **Do Not Call Attention to Yourself!** If you forget all the rules, just remember not to call attention to yourself. Follow the behavior of your host or whoever in your setting is the leader. Better not to be noticed than to be remembered for terrible etiquette (to start with, turn off your cell phone ringer!). Let your intelligence, talent, and ability to help others be how people know you!

3. **Smile & Make Eye Contact!** A smile is a sign of happiness. And people naturally want happiness in their lives. Your eyes are connected to your smile. Folks trust people who look them in the eye. What people look at indicates their interest. Looking someone in the eye is the easiest way to show your interest and sincerity.

4. **Early is On Time!** Early is on time, on time is late, and late is left behind. Leaders are always where they are supposed to be, doing what they are supposed to be doing, when they are supposed to be doing it. Respect time and you will prevent issues and promote yourself to great responsibility.

5. **Never Greet from Your Seat!** It doesn't matter who you meet in life, show them respect by rising to meet them.

6. **Gossip About the Success of Others**! In today's world of negative news it seems everyone is talking about everyone else. If you must speak of others, speak of the good they do, their success and nothing else.

7. **Be Pressed & Polished!** Styles come and go. But, wearing outfits that fit, coordinated, clean, and pressed along with shoes that are polished never goes out of fashion.

8. **Mind Your Table Manners!** Never is etiquette more on display then when you are dining. Chewing with your mouth closed, elbows off the table, and waiting until everyone is served to begin eating is just the start!

9. **Turn the "M" Upside Down!** Leaders talk about "we" not "me." They turn the "M" into a "W" and use inclusive language. Watch how much you use the terms "I", "me", or "my" and adjust to "us", "our' and "we".

10. **Give Thanks!** Whether someone gives you a physical gift or the more precious prize of their time, energy, support, and help, show your appreciation through thoughtful thanks. A handwritten "thank you" that is specific about your appreciation is never a waste of time.

By following the etiquette code you develop your own personal brand. People remember you cared enough make others feel warm, welcome, and comfortable. In turn they remember you, your family, and the organizations you represent in a positive way. And simply put, people will want to be around you because you create a positive environment filled with gracious and respectful people.

The Dos and Don'ts of Modern Communication

By Leslie Becker-Phelps, PhD

When I read some of the unnecessarily harsh comments people post on news articles or blogs (thankfully, not usually mine), I become concerned for our collective future. When the cashier at a store is too busy texting to acknowledge my existence, I find myself put off and, again, concerned. And I don't even want to get started on when I see people texting and driving.

So, I was happy when I recently had the opportunity to chat with Thomas P. Farley, a New York-based manners and lifestyle expert. His website, whatmannersmost.com, provides all kinds of interesting and useful information about contemporary etiquette. He could relate to my concerns and talked about how people's use of technology often constitutes bad manners and causes problems in relationships. With this in mind, he shared the following "dos and don'ts" of communicating through technology:

Do: Turn off your cell phone when you are with others and give them your full attention. If you need to have it on because you are awaiting a very important call, let them know right up front.

Don't: Give more attention to cell phones than people. This is rude and gives people the message that they are not important. In addition, constant texting means you are never really involved in your current interaction. Mr. Farley highlighted this point by noting that someone might not be attending to a conversation because he is texting about plans for dinner, and then arrives at that dinner where he begins to text to make plans for something else.

Do: When commenting on blog posts or bulletin boards, be sure that your comments are constructive. You can certainly disagree or make critical statements, but this should be done in a constructive and not unduly harsh way.

Don't: Be mean-spirited. People too often use their anonymity to say things they would never say in person. Unfortunately, because people are getting used to being less-than-sensitive or have been the recipients of mean statements, this style of communication is trickling out to other interactions – which, of course, is not good for any relationships.

Do: Make every effort to respond to personal communications in personal ways.

Don't: Overuse texting. People often return phone calls or emails with texts – and not just when they are in circumstances where it is clearly preferable, such as at concerts or on the train. While it's a quick, efficient way of responding, it also is less personal and keeps relationships more distant.

Do: Write clearly to help ensure that you are expressing yourself well.

Don't: Overuse abbreviations. This keeps people from practicing their spelling and from writing clear, articulate messages. The result is that people don't learn to, or get out of practice with, communicating effectively. It can put them at a disadvantage in getting their points across, which can be a particular liability at many jobs.

Do: Make sure that you give thought to, and exert effort with, your close friends.

Don't: Maintain a vast number of "friends" on social networking sites if it means you wind up spending less time forging close meaningful relationships. Keeping up with a large network of people — though valuable from a business and networking standpoint — takes time and energy. The unfortunate result is often that in their race to rack up virtual acquaintances, many people begin to neglect their real friends; the ones who will be there for them in times of need, and who will give them a deeper sense of connection.

As Mr. Farley finished sharing his thoughts, he explained that people who choose to do these things are respected and liked. And, he added (with an enthusiasm that I really liked), "When you are kind to other people, it comes back to you; AND IT FEELS GOOD."

TIME MANAGEMENT SKILLS TEST

One of the greatest factors contributing to stress is our inability to manage time.

Conversely, good time management skills allow us to organize our lives and be more productive, both at work and at home.

The following quiz will help identify trouble spots and guide us toward the goal of becoming successful time managers.

A scoring key at the end will indicate how far you need to go. Assign a numerical number to the following questions with l=always; 2=usually; 3=sometimes; 4=never.

____ I find that I have enough time for myself to do the things I enjoy doing.

____ I'm aware of deadlines and schedule my work to meet them in time.

____ I write down specific objectives in order to work toward goals.

____ I use a calendar to write down appointments, deadlines, and things to do.

____ I feel in control of time while at work and at home.

____ I plan and schedule my time on a weekly and/or monthly basis.

____ I make a daily to-do list and refer to it several times per day.

____ I set priorities in order of importance and then schedule time around them.

____ I'm able to find time when I need it in case something important comes up.

____ I'm able to say no when I'm pressed for time.

____ I try to delegate responsibility to others in order to make more time for myself.

____ I organize my desk and work area to prevent clutter and confusion.

____ I find it easy to eliminate or reschedule low priority items.

____ I try to do things in a way that cuts down on duplicated effort.

____ I find that doing everything myself is very inefficient.

____ I try to shift priorities as soon as they change.

____ I find it easy to identify sources of time problems.

___ I find it easy to eliminate or reshuffle unnecessary paperwork.

___ My meetings and activities are well organized and efficient.

___ I know what I'm capable of and try not to overextend myself.

___ I find it easy to keep up with changes that affect my schedule or workload.

___ I try to schedule the most difficult work during my most productive times.

___ I know what my responsibilities and duties are at all times.

___ I try to get only the pertinent information before making a final decision.

___ I finish one job or task before going on to the next.

Scoring key:

25 - 40 = Excellent time manager

41 - 55 = Good time manager

56 - 100 = Poor time manager

If you scored above 55, you have lots of work to do in order to become an effective time manager and avoid the stress that leads to productivity problems, stress, burnout, and disease. The most common areas to look for are:

-Not prioritizing tasks

-Not scheduling daily, weekly, or monthly activities

-Not delegating responsibility

-Not being able to say no

-Not writing down objectives in order to meet deadlines

-Not using a calendar or notebook to organize commitments

-Not shifting priorities to make room for more urgent matters or tasks

-Not reducing clutter and/or unnecessary paperwork

-Not being able to give up total control

-Not being able to avoid procrastination

Notes:

Notes:

Made in the USA
Coppell, TX
18 June 2021